Jenny L. Lewis

PAGE PUBLISHING
Conneaut Lake, PA

First originally published by Page Publishing 2024

ISBN 979-8-89553-058-0 (pbk)
ISBN 979-8-89553-069-6 (digital)

Printed in the United States of America

Thank you to the love of my life, my best friend, and my biggest cheerleader. Benjy, this wouldn't be possible without you always believing in me and never letting me give up. You heard me doubt myself time and time again, but your confidence in me and my work never wavered. Thank you to the ones who inspired my work. Without the disappointment and heartbreak you caused, I would have never been able to learn valuable lessons and make our stories known. And lastly, to the ones who can relate to these experiences, I see you. I hear you. You are worthy.

Like wildflowers, you must allow yourself to grow in
all the places people thought you never would.

i don't wish you the best

i wish you the worst

i hope you're reminded of my absence

when you're lying in bed at night trying to fall asleep

i hope you miss our late nights together, laughing and holding
      each other tight

i hope you miss them when you're

at the kitchen table, trying to eat as the children fight

the children you now call your own

call it pride, pity, or selfishness

call it what you will

i hope the thought of me and what we were makes you ill

i wish you the worst

my body and mind were never in sync
they have forever been enemies
fighting a war within my body
one that neither will ever win
until one day, they joined forces and realized
they are one in the same
both battered, sick, and broken

my favorite time of day is when you're near me
the day is ending, the sky is turning beautiful shades of pink and
	orange
we sit and talk about our day
i absorb every word you say
i can't help but think to myself
damn, this is love

the tires of your rusted pontiac stop on the gravel
i know i need to quickly exit the car before my father sees us
but i don't want to
i take a deep breath and move my hand towards the door's
    handle
suddenly, the doors lock
next our eyes, and lastly
our mouths
and this is where our story officially starts
at the beginning

all i smell is espresso

i hear machines working in tandem

it's a miracle that i can hear anything besides the pumping

of my blood in my heart

it's in my chest, my veins, all the way up to the drums in my ears

it's crowded, but my memory couldn't place a face even if i tried

all i can see is you

it's like tunnel vision, with no light at the end

i know all i'll find is darkness

it's at this pivotal moment that i know you will break me

and i don't care because i want you all the same

i force my feet to move, one foot in front of the other towards
 you

towards the tunnel that will undoubtably become my new
 residence

all i smell is espresso

all i see is you

your lips on my neck
your hand between my thighs
i'm where i've always wanted to be
but never been before
home

tidbits from me to you

your life is a collection of rotating seasons, and some things are only meant to last through so many of them. you can't make it snow in the summer, even if winter is your favorite time of the year.

love

she's fierce, fickle, demanding, and above all
intentional and always with purpose
i spent over a decade of my life believing i was in love
believing what i felt was as good as unconditional love could get
and then it happened
you ran your fingers through my hair as i lay next to you
i was silent, but my mind was very much screaming loudly
i lay there, feeling a foreign emotion
that's when it hit me
this is love

we sat in the living room we arranged together
you had your legs up on the coffee table that i just had to have
my mouth spoke the words that my heart and brain couldn't
for the last few years
your eyes reached mine, every emotion spiraling within those baby
    blues
you walked away as you lost your lunch in our guest bathroom
the bathroom we decorated together
after years of efforts, requests, pleas
there's only one thing left that i often think about
i miss that coffee table

i'm the happiest i've ever been
i'm the saddest i've ever been
i've acquired pure, genuine, honest love
but by doing so, i must grieve the loss of another type of love
a friendship, a partnership, a decade worth of memories
i'm the happiest i've ever been
i'm the saddest i've ever been

the music to our favorite band plays
it's a welcome tune, after almost two years
depriving myself of it
i can listen to it now and the grief of memories is just a very
    distant emotion
it's still there, like a distant cousin you only see once a year
all the same
just like us

stop putting yourself out there for people
who couldn't care less and wouldn't do the same
you deserve better, you deserve to shine
and to be amongst people that admire that shine
and want to make it brighter and more beautiful
beautiful, like you

my grandmother was one of the most beautiful women i've ever
    known
hair always curled, nails painted, and makeup just right
as a child, she would always paint my nails
she'd have the lightest touch
it was one of the many ways in which we bonded, i loved it so
    much
she never let me paints her though, she said i was too young
days before she left this earth and me, she asked me to paint
    her nails
she did correct me a few times, she told me two coats were just too
    light
after we were done, she thanked me with love in her eyes
and we both knew it was almost her time
she was one of the most beautiful women i've ever known

you can't tell me I don't have the right to be heartbroken
just because I was the one who walked away
you can't tell me I can't mourn a life that I once had
just because I chose to not live it anymore

you would bend me until I broke if I let you
shattered and splintered
all my cells spread out
like an emotional kaleidoscope throughout my body
and I would thank you
I'd ask you to do it again

there's a fine line between lust and love
infatuation and adoration
temptation and obsession
when it comes to you, the lines are blurred
like faded ink on a piece of paper
i'd ask you for one night, to spread me wide
open me up and let the emotions spill out
one night wouldn't subdue them though
an entire lifetime couldn't accomplish that

it was a spark, a small flicker of light when we would talk

then you touched me, and it was an explosion

you were all around me

you overwhelmed my senses, i couldn't breathe or speak

in an instant, i was putty in your hands

you asked me if i wanted to see you again after this night, and
who was i to say no

the next morning, i watched you put on your black combat
boots

fresh out of the shower, while i lay in your bed

with your scent surrounding me

i came back for seconds, and even thirds until i realized i was
just another name in your book, another notch in that
very long belt that you had

i didn't matter, and i never would have

the rhythm of drumsticks on a cymbal had nothing on the beat
    of my heart
i wasn't gone in sixty seconds, i was gone in ten
i opened the door to get to you, and without any control
i opened my heart
and just as quickly, the sticks lit fire
the cymbals turned to dust
and i was alone

i stop and think, i can't be mad at you

i started this, you see

i had questions, you had the answers

it was as simple as could be

how would i know meeting you would have me questioning
everything i wanted

and nothing i needed

to your charismatic ways, your charming smile

it led me to your kind eyes, your husky voice, the dimple in
your cheeks

it led me down a road, to the left, and straight towards
disappointment and heartache

tidbits from me to you

time is not relevant when it comes to your happiness. we only have so much time in this life. live the shit out of it.

it was late at night, and i was eight

i was eight when my father chose his life over mine

while i was at the neighbor's house playing

he was taking his chance with a bridge and a rifle

while i sat there, wondering what my father and i would

do together tomorrow

he was wondering what it would feel like if all the pain was

erased

fast-forward to the next morning

my father was home, but we wouldn't be spending time together

i'd be spending time learning what he did and forever feeling

terrified he'd try again

my friend bought me bubble tea the other day

it was a kind surprise, i couldn't say no

all the while all it made me think of was you

the flavor hit my tongue and my body reacted instantaneously

my stomach was sore, my intestines twisting and turning

my chest felt the weight of one hundred bricks being balance
    on top of it

then i remembered

i remembered who i am and who you are not

who you were and who you will never be

i thanked my friend with kind eyes and a smile

never letting either waver

i drank it as quickly as i could

she thought i loved the taste

when all i really wanted was to get the memory of you out of my
    system

as quickly as i could

the smell of lilacs remind me of home

they remind me of a painted white porch, with painted white
    rocks

rocks that i used to love to play on

the smell of lilac is love, security, and freedom

freedom from the chaos of my parents

chaos that was their marriage, and consequently my life

my favorite smell is, and will always be, lilac

i was six when the strings in my brain snapped

and new ones were created in the place

i was six when i learned a closet can hold more than clothes

more than skeletons, it can hold memories and secrets

memories that my subconscious graciously hid and protected
     me from until i was ready

it took those memories, stored them in a box with a lock and
     key to ensure the box was closed

i was six when the new strings were created in their place

a closet isn't where you find clothes to put on, it's where you
     have them removed

i was six when my innocence was taken from me

my arms were planted firmly on the floor, my legs spread wide

i was six when new strings had to be created

i like to write down words that i cannot say
it helps me get through each and every day
it's easier to let my emotions spill on a piece of paper rather than
allowing myself to bleed these emotions in front of you
it's funny though, you'll read them and not have a clue
they are all about you

tidbits from me to you

let go of that self-hatred and guilt and choose yourself. you're worth it, i promise.

i was freshly sixteen and i was ready
you waited through the last two years
through the miles that separate us
i knew i was ready
this was love after all, right?
you hand me a glass bottle with red liquid in it
you tell me to take a few sips, it'll calm my nerves
it'll quiets any doubts i may have, smooth out the insecurities
    that have begun to seep in
it burns like acid down my throat, but i drink it all
i do it for you
because we are in love
i know this because you reminded me just the other day
the liquid is gone and i'm tired
you cover me up with a blanket, tuck me in nice and snug
you must truly love me
the last thing i remember is smiling up at you
and then there's darkness
my eyes open in the morning and i'm on the floor

i see bruises on my body and the place between my legs is sore
i hear the pitter-patter of your feet coming up the stairs
you open the door with toast and orange juice
the toast is burnt, and the orange juice is sour on my tongue
you tell me i'm a good girl, that i made you happy
an hour later, i'm in the shower counting my bruises
formulating a plan to hide them from the world
my stomach aches and the toast is now splattered on the shower
    floor
i stay in the shower until my body is numb and my fingers are
    pruned
my heart and head concluded that this is the end
you let me know you'd be right back, that your errands wouldn't
    take long
i waited and waited
four years later and i finally understood
and trust me, i would also leave me if i could

it was an ordinary night for us

i was on the couch with our dogs, and you playing video games
with our closest friends

i hear your laugh that i've always loved and for some reason

i have the desire to be closer to you, the space between rooms
seems to be too much

i haven't felt this way in a while, so i'm surprised and truly happy
about this

we've fallen into a routine, our life is stagnant as of late, and i
find myself longing for more

i stop to use the bathroom, excited to spend the rest of the night
near you

when something tells me to check the cabinet above the toilet

i'll never be able to explain it, this pull that my brain had

it was sudden, and there was no ignoring it

as i stood on the toilet, my stomach filled with dread and
disappointment

i grab the half-empty liquor bottle that has been hidden from me

you promised me you'd get better, and i thought you were

i was so proud, ever the supporter

this moment was pivotal, it was the moment that i knew

we shared a few tears and i was honest about my fears

even after all these years, i knew we'd never be the same

cheers to five years
cheers to a cheap ring, a vegas wedding, and a twenty-dollar
    dress
shortly after, my mind became a mess
this is as good as it gets though, right?
so i buckled up tight and settled for what
would be the rest of my life

i decided i'd stay quiet, i'd let people believe the story you created

the story that painted you as the victim

you made yourself the main character in this story

you chose the beginning, middle, and end

this was a masterpiece, a true work of art

it was abstract, mesmerizing, and everyone wanted to buy it

after about a month, it sold out

all copies were bought, some even had to be pre-ordered

so all that's left to do is congratulate you, you're officially an
    author

the moon and stars don't hold a candle to you
you're extraordinary, truly one of a kind
it's a miracle that i can call you mine
you came into my life and took over all the darkness with your
    light
it shone so bright that i had no control over the magnitude of it
it was beautiful, just like you, and just like us

not having the ability to have a baby in your womb
does not make you less of a woman
making the choice to not have a baby in your womb
does not make you less of a woman
your choices, your own mind,
using both of those freely
that's what makes you a woman

you were never my soulmate

and i was never yours

that doesn't mean i didn't love you with everything i could

this doesn't mean i didn't try to give you everything i had to
offer at that time

we were never going to fit though

our life was a puzzle that could never be completed

always missing pieces that could never be found

tidbits from me to you

you are never too much for someone; they are simply not
enough for you.

for every bottle that was supposed to be your last but never
     really was
for every apology i gave because i felt like my world would
     shatter if i didn't
for every accusation i'd receive for having a drink with a friend
for every moment that i was enjoying myself, letting my
     personality shine, and you told me i was too much
that light within me dimmed each time you spoke those words
     and by the end, the bulb didn't just flicker, it was burnt out

like most stories go when you're nineteen and naive, this one
     starts with a boy
there was a boy in a band who asked me to come to his show
he watched me the entire time he played
the crowd didn't have his attention, nor did his bandmates
it was me who did
after the show, he came to sit next to me and a friend
the other girls were envious, each one wanting it to be them
     your charming smile was for
that night, we discovered each other's bodies while a movie
     played in the background
he gently kissed each one of my tattoos, asking what each one meant
we spent the rest of the night learning each other's minds and
     warming his small twin-size bed
that night, i fell in love with a boy in a band with long blond
     hair, who liked to wear combat boots and a leather jacket
     to work in the morning

tidbits from me to you

embrace your imperfections, quirks, and flaws. they have transformed you into who you truly are, and that's a pretty badass human being.

intimacy to you is nothing more than a transaction
one you would wish to have a subscription to if you could
you'd subscribe monthly, because yearly is too much of a
    commitment

i'll never forget the day you told me you didn't love my soul
you told me you loved my body
my mind and thoughts didn't matter to you, all you cared about
    was taking any opportunity you could
to use me, make me feel important for a short while
once you had your fill, you'd leave and i'd feel empty and alone
there were times i had hope
those would be the times you would say how extraordinary i was
how you couldn't wait to see me again after so many years
you fooled me time and time again and i let you
until one day i realized, it's okay that you don't love my soul
it's okay because you didn't have one to begin with

b.d.h.

two years together and i still look at you and can't believe you're
    mine
ten years will go by, and i will always think the same thing
your soul is the kindest, your voice will always make me
    smile, and the way your body fits perfectly with mine is
    something i will cherish for years to come
if soulmates are real, our souls were made for each other
if they are real, yours and mine are the same

About the Author

Jenny has always had two main passions in life, writing and animals. She has worked in the veterinary field and has done so for over five years. As a child, she would write short stories for her classmates to read, and as she became older, her interest moved toward poetry. She uses poetry as a way to express her emotions, dreams, and life experiences. In her free time, she loves to read dark romance novels and spend time with her little zoo of a family.